ROCKS

by Robin Nelson

first step nonfiction

Lerner Publications Company · Minneapolis

We live on Earth.

Earth is made of
different things.

Earth is made of water,
gases, soil, and rocks.

Most of Earth is made
of **rock.**

Rocks are hard.

Rocks can be
different shapes.

Rocks can be different sizes.

Rocks can be different colors.

Boulders are big rocks.

Pebbles are small rocks.

Sand is made of tiny rocks.

Some rocks have **metal**
in them.

People build statues
with rocks.

People build roads
with rocks.

Some houses are made
with rocks.

Rocks are found on Earth.

Three Kinds of Rocks

Igneous rocks are melted deep in the ground. Over time, they cool and harden.

Sedimentary rocks are made from bits of dead plants, animals or tiny rocks. They pile in layers and then harden.

Metamorphic rocks are heated and squeezed in the ground so much, they change into a different rock.

Rock Types

Igneous

granite

Sedimentary

marble

Metamorphic

sandstone

Rare Rock Facts

 Earth's surface is made of rock. Most of the rock is hidden under soil and water.

 The oldest rocks are almost four billion years old. That is almost as old as Earth!

 Some kinds of rock are so light they can float.

 It took fourteen years to carve the faces on Mount Rushmore. They are 60 feet tall and the noses are 20 feet long.

Moving water can change the shape of rocks. It washes part of the rock away and makes it smooth.

 Very hot and cold temperatures can make rocks change and crack.

 Many fossils are animals or plants that died long ago and turned into rock.

 Birds eat small pieces of stone to help them digest food they eat.

Glossary

 boulders – large rounded rocks

 metal – something found in the ground that is shiny and hard

 pebbles – small round stones

 rock – a hard object in the ground

 sand – tiny bits of worn rock

Index

The photographs in this book are reproduced through the courtesy of: PhotoDisc Royalty Free by Getty Images, cover, pp. 19 (inset, top), 19 (inset, middle); © LWA-Dann Tardif/CORBIS, p.2; NASA, p. 3; © Randy Wells/CORBIS p. 4; [Collection], U.S. Geological Survey Photo Library p. 5; © Royalty-Free/CORBIS, p. 6; © Gordon Whitten/CORBIS, pp. 7, 8, 22 (second from bottom); © Peter Johnson/CORBIS, p. 9; © David Muench/CORBIS, pp. 10, 22 (top); © Brendan Curran/Independent Picture Service, pp. 11, 22 (middle); © Doug Crouch/CORBIS, pp. 12, 22 (bottom); © Phil Schermeister/CORBIS, pp. 13, 22 (second from top); © Peter Beck/CORBIS, p. 14; © Darrell Gulin/CORBIS, p. 15; © Liba Taylor/CORBIS, p. 16; © WildCountry/CORBIS, p. 17; © Tom Bean/CORBIS p. 19 (top); Jonathan Blair/CORBIS p. 19 (middle); Owen Franken/ CORBIS p. 19 (bottom); © Jeff Vanuga/CORBIS p. 19 (inset, bottom).

Lerner Publications Company
A division of Lerner Publishing Group
241 First Avenue North
Minneapolis, MN 55401 U.S.A.

Website address: www.lernerbooks.com

Library of Congress Cataloging-in-Publication Data

Nelson, Robin, 1971–
    Rocks / by Robin Nelson.
        p.   cm. — (First step nonfiction)
    Includes index.
    ISBN: 0–8225–2599–2 (lib. bdg. : alk. paper)
    1. Rocks—Juvenile literature. 2. Petrology—Juvenile literature. I. Title. II. Series.
QE432.2.N45 2005
    552—dc22   2004020785

Manufactured in the United States of America
1 2 3 4 5 6 – DP – 10 09 08 07 06 05